Winter of My Life

Winter of My Life

Poems by

Sherri Wright

© 2024 Sherri Wright. All rights reserved.
This material may not be reproduced in any form, published,
reprinted, recorded, performed, broadcast,
rewritten, or redistributed without
the explicit permission of Sherri Wright.
All such actions are strictly prohibited by law.

Cover design by Shay Culligan
Cover image by Richard Byrne
Author photo by Angie Moon Photography

ISBN: 978-1-63980-665-2
Library of Congress Control Number: 2024949542

Kelsay Books
502 South 1040 East, A-119
American Fork, Utah 84003
Kelsaybooks.com

Acknowledgments

Thanks to the following journals and anthologies in which these poems appeared, sometimes in slightly different versions:

Clementine: "If Today"
Decimos We Say, Voices of the Florida Keys: "Skeletons of Old Town Key West"
Delaware Beach Life: "On Moving to a Small Town"
The Divine Feminine, An Anthology of Seaside Scribes: "The Garden Goddess"
Dreamer's Creative Writing: "When You Write My Eulogy"
Letters From Camp Rehoboth: "Waiting for Sunrise"
Panoplyzine: "Joint Custody"
Prairie Schooner: "Private Dancer"
Quartet: "Elizabeth Bishop Invites Me In"
Rat's Ass Review: "I Want a New Running Skirt"
Rehoboth Beach Writer's Guild Anthology: "The Great Blue Heron at Silver Lake"
Tiny Seed Literary Journal: "I Can't Mend the Coral Reef"

Thanks to Maribeth Fischer and the Rehoboth Beach Writers Guild for teaching me and supporting my writing. A special thank you to Gail Comorat who encouraged me and helped pull together this collection. And who, with Ethan Joella, taught me everything I know about poetry.

Contents

Elizabeth Bishop Invites Me In	11
I Want a New Running Skirt	12
Comfort Food	13
The Face in the Mirror	15
1969	17
She Worked Late	18
I Have Forgotten	20
Joint Custody	22
Private Dancer	23
The Garden Goddess	24
Falling Is No Disgrace: *a pandemic glosa after lines from "So Many Ways to Do It Right" by Rosemerry Wahtola Trommer*	25
4-H Lament	27
I Can't Mend the Coral Reef	28
The Great Blue Heron at Silver Lake	30
Hay Creek Cemetery	32
Skeletons in Old Town Key West	34
Osprey's Return Ghazal	36
White Porcelain Vase	37
On Moving to a Small Town	38
Waiting for Sunrise	39
They Sit Together on the Deck	40
Love Poem After Thirty-Seven Years	41
I Write Her Name in the Sand	43
Autumnal Equinox	45
When You Write My Eulogy	46
Brushing the Dog	47
If Today	48

Elizabeth Bishop Invites Me In

Morning run, sweat pearling, sliding down my face.
In the front door of the old eyebrow house, Elizabeth
smiles, motions, I follow her in. Cool, sparse,
high ceilings. A fan hums. Book lined walls.
She hands me water in a crystal glass. Points
to a chair. I swallow politely, try not to gulp.
We talk about writing. About Key West.
I see dilapidated houses, palms slapping tin roofs,
iguanas feeding on orchids and frangipani.
Black roosters don't let me sleep. She sees sheer water,
turquoise tarpons, fork-tailed frigate birds
soaring silent. The crash of pelicans like pick axes.
Elizabeth tells me she came to Key West to fish.
Like Hemingway.
Fish, silver and iridescent in blue water.
A large fish she caught and let go, five hooks
in its mouth. And poetry. Elizabeth tells me
this is a beautiful place to write.

I Want a New Running Skirt

I want a new running skirt
short and tight in a bright purple
print I want to wear
that skirt with a tank that bares
my shoulders leaves my arms free
to swing in synch with my flying feet

I want to feel the heat of the sun
the wet of sweat rolling down
my back I want to run
in that skirt through Delmarva past
North Carolina beyond Savannah
and Miami Beach I want that skirt
to get me away from long pants
fleece vests wooly hats and gloves

In that skirt I will leave the dread
of swabs and tests and toxins in the air
the terror of touching a hand
when I hand groceries to someone
who has never before asked for food

I want that skirt to carry me past
the agony of bodies in parking lots
waiting for a gurney or a hospital bed
beyond the horror of guns and clubs
blood stains on marble steps

I need this skirt to assuage
the panic that whispers in the night
nothing will ever be the way it was
I need something to allay
the fear of never seeing my kids again

Comfort Food

Comfort food: simply prepared, digestible, un-sophisticated food that is psychologically comforting, especially food high in carbohydrates.
—Encarta Dictionary

In these ambiguous days I crave
the goulash my mother used to make
when we lived on the farm
the aroma of onions and celery
browning with peppers and ground beef
sizzling in a cast iron pan
she never called it comfort food
it was just routine
two quarts of canned tomatoes
and a box of elbow macaroni
stretched out a pound of meat
to feed six kids

I long for the bread pudding
she used to bake from a torn up loaf
of homemade bread   the scent
of cinnamon in scalded milk wafting
up the stairs
comforting the kitchen
on cold winter afternoons
baked crusty on top
custardy below and served
warm with cream

My mother didn't think about calories
or carbs she just needed to fill bellies
of hungry boys who milked cows
and gathered eggs before school
and the skinny girl who fed the baby
and washed dishes
while her mother was out in the barn

I need to fill my belly with food
that increases the serotonin level in my brain
makes me feel good   I am hungry
with a nostalgia that makes my stomach rumble
and gives me dreams
of my mother   of her goulash
of her bread pudding
served warm with cream

The Face in the Mirror

In the mirror you stare at your mother's face
But this is not the woman who taught you to sew
or sang in the choir in the little Methodist church
not the woman who lived on a farm   birthed
eight children   milked cows   washed clothes
and hung them on the line   who pulled cinnamon rolls
out of the oven just when you and your brothers
came home from school

Nor is this the woman married 75 years
to the same man   following his career
walking two steps behind   ironing
his shirts   Not the woman who knitted
booties for every baby   sweaters
for every toddler and teen   who served
every birthday every graduation every Christmas Eve
and dinner for anyone who dropped in

No   you are the woman who had one child
and daycare   a college degree and a career
the woman who moved from city to city
to get ahead in your job   had an affair
a divorce   fought for joint custody   marched
for women's rights   you didn't iron shirts
for any man   and you could never
explain to your mother why you didn't
settle down and come back home

When you were young   people said
you looked just like your mother
but you couldn't see it   she had brown hair
and hazel eyes   you were blue eyed and blonde
but now   in this mirror   hair graying
eyes faded to neither hazel nor blue   skin creasing
and lining like the rings of an old oak
no matter how hard you tried
you still see your mother's face in the mirror

1969

We wore bell bottom pants low at the waist
tight on the thighs and flared to high heaven
with flimsy tank tops instead of bras
we traded high heels for clunky leather sandals
smoothed our teased and sprayed hair let it grow down our backs
the straighter and blonder the better
we donned love beads and dream catcher
earrings and sometimes a paisley
headband but never dared a tattoo we walked barefoot
along the beach moved to music in the park
on summer nights too hot for third floor apartments
and campus housing we craved
that casual look our mothers would
have frowned upon and that we couldn't
pull off in our teaching lives it was that carefree
season when the world opened new

She Worked Late

She worked late every night since her husband
was gone and always enjoyed the short walk
from the Metro station home. This evening
the sun turned the old stone townhouses
warm copper and the apple blossom air invited
a leisurely pace on the cobblestone street
she'd walked so many nights before.

At an intersection close to home she met
two boys who looked to be in their teens,
they veered, she nodded and walked on.
She was thinking about a glass of wine and a salad
she'd be eating alone when she heard a low voice

> *"drop it"*
> *"drop it"*

A flash of silver was all she saw she didn't think
she just screamed and ran her heart hammering
her briefcase tight in her fist dogs barking a car screeching
to a halt at the curb an undercover cop
who'd been following those two all evening

Staring at two skinny boys handcuffed
and squinting under the glare of a spotlight
her life work flashed by her   a haze of

>   research
>   reports
>   speeches
>   justice
>   equality

It wasn't academic any more here she was
face to face with the *high-risk kids*
she'd worked late for every night

She didn't think of positive outcomes or learning
opportunities for these boys as she sat shaking
in the unmarked car with the visor pulled low
so she could identify them and not be seen.

Her work hadn't prepared her

for
        trial
        testimony
        prosecutors
        public defenders
        scowling boys
        sullen mothers in the court room

or

        the broken glass
        the brick through her kitchen window

I Have Forgotten

I have forgotten your thick
horn rimmed glasses grinning
brown eyes under a coil of blond hair
I have no memory of a party
my freshman year with my
girlfriend and my brother or you
driving me home that rainy night
I don't recall meeting you every day
skipping Psych 101 to drive to St. Croix
and climb the rocky ledges I have no recall
of biology lessons in the front seat
of your souped-up Studebaker red leather
seats stick shift between our legs I don't remember
being eager to go all the way or drop out of school
and get married so I could sleep
with you every night I don't recall asking
why I worked at the pharmacy to pay
your tuition and rent for that drab trailer house
I tried to cheer up with ruffled curtains
and the smell of baking bread I have no memory
of you teaching me to bait a fish hook or shoot
a twenty two rifle I remember
nothing of camping or carrying a Duluth pack as big as
a St Bernard portaging to lakes so pure
we could bathe in and drink the same water

I don't remember leaving for Ithaca
with a new car a new degree and a job teaching first grade
I don't recall new friends jug wine concerts in the park
anti war protests sit-ins in the armory I have no memory
of graduate school and the baby born
the same day I finished my thesis
the baby we both wanted the baby
whose hands were yours whose eyes were mine
the little girl we rocked and sang to and strolled to
Stuart Park on summer nights too hot
for our third floor apartment
and I really don't remember
why we didn't make this work

Joint Custody

At three fifteen my office phone will ring
as she drops books and shoes at the front door.
She's breathless. *Can I open a can of soup? Can I
watch TV? Can Annie come over and do homework?*
She knows the rule about friends
when I'm not home. I hear the refrigerator slam
and the theme from Happy Days and she's gone
before I can tell her what to take out for supper.

How did we end up like this I wonder, looking at her
in ankle length cotton skirt safety pinned at the waist
over long johns and a tie-dyed tee. Through deep teal
lined eyes she teases me that her whole Rag Stock
wardrobe cost less than one of my suits. And her stark
bi-level haircut was free. Somehow every other week
morphed into three out of four and then full time. I max out
my credit cards.

Come summer I take her on work trips with the promise
of a hotel pool and a Dairy Queen. Teach her to take the city bus
from our apartment to day camp and art class. We read
Maya Angelou and Rita Mae Brown. I drag her
to my soccer games rallies for women's rights invite her friends
to come along. We sing I Am Woman Hear Me Roar. She leads
a student protest. Am I making her grow up too soon?

Like marionettes we are dancing proud independent
arms bobbing on our little stage feet stepping lithely
between what is and what was supposed to be heads not asking
for anything more not knowing that soon it will be necessary
to sever our own strings.

Private Dancer

I'll buy a black leather mini skirt
like the one Tina Turner wore
when she sang Private Dancer in 1979.
that pelt will fit like the
rind of an orange over the curve of my hips,
It will twist and talk
with every move. I'll yank
that skirt over a little tank top
fringed in sequins and beads that shiver
and shimmer with every exhale. I'll dance
long bronze legs into my
daughter's classroom, rock past the hippie teacher
and roll right up to the smarty friend
who lives in the big house on the lake. That girl
who walked into my bathroom,
helped herself to my lipstick and polish
and was amazed that my daughter and I
cooked dinner, set a table, and sat down to eat.
With my little mini, I will shimmy,
into the office of the counselor who wrote
"broken home" into my 3rd grader's
permanent file. I will close the door
swivel my hips onto his desk, look him
in the eye, I will teach him what a "divorcée" looks like,
any music will do.

The Garden Goddess

Aphrodite stands proud among the maiden hair ferns. Her clay neck is scarred and her arm wears a canvas sling. The man and woman of the house had found her in the morning lying in the rose bushes next to the gate. They patched her broken arm with mortar and cemented her back onto her pedestal. She heard the pity in their voices as they blamed the storm that had downed branches and toppled trees on the boulevard. They wouldn't think to ask a goddess where she'd been. And they wouldn't have believed her if she'd told them how she'd scaled the fence and sashayed down to Eighth street for a change of scenery last night. She was bored with the doves and sparrows and rhododendrons that had no personalities. At the first disco she'd let down her toga, danced nude on the tables, laughed as the men clapped, called her *ecstasy* and asked to take her home. But, like Cinderella she had to leave before dawn and get back to her garden. She had to be on the pedestal and have the urn in her hand before the woman came out for the morning paper. In her rush, she'd tripped over that damn dress, hit the pavement, and broken her arm. No, the wind or the thunder hadn't crushed her bones but she didn't regret the wine, the music, the men, the sip of life—and who was she to spoil their myth?

Falling Is No Disgrace: *a pandemic glosa after lines from "So Many Ways to Do It Right" by Rosemerry Wahtola Trommer*

*So this is what it takes
to notice the beauty of being still,
to see how staying in place, too, is a path,
how falling, too, is a grace.*

So this is what it takes
to see your world as it really is:
a microscopic organism in the system
to reveal festering wounds of neglect
expose the ingrained pain of prejudice.
This is what it takes to admit the mistakes
to face the fight, wrestle the resistance,
to change the structure, to shatter
the shield that privilege stakes,
before the country splinters and breaks.

To notice the beauty of being still
in a year of closures and cancels
staying at home, finding the silence
where once you heard music and laughter,
the voices of your children. Now only
the tap of the cat treading the sill,
greening of leaves outside the window,
a wave washing the shore,
a setting sun before evening's chill,
these small things leave you fulfilled.

To see how staying in place, too, is a path
though not the one you would have chosen
had not this alien creature, enveloped
your daylight and devoured your dreams
with equal measure of fear and trepidation
and forced you to tread a wide swath
beyond the fences of your comfort and ease,
shown you the ravages of deprivation,
and lead you through the trails of wrath,
rage, and fury left in its aftermath.

How falling, too, is a grace
if you can lift yourself upright,
reach out for what was nearly lost,
pick up the pieces that warrant repair,
unravel the roots of iniquity woven into the fabric.
Falling, too, is a grace if a person will embrace
another's hurt, walk in her shoes, feel her fear,
and catch her if she falls. Let her know
you journey together in this arduous race
and falling is no disgrace.

4-H Lament

I toggle between pages of the Washington Post. Page 4: After review by parent committees Toni Morrison's *Bluest Eye, To Kill a Mockingbird* by Harper Lee, *New Kid* by Jerry Craft, *Stamped* by Reynolds and Kendi struck from school libraries. Page 5: a Chicago based gun manufacturer unveils their child-size JR-15 assault rife, designed expressly for children, marketed directly to children via a girl in pigtails.

young children
reading in meadows
unaware of land mines

It brings back a 4-H meeting years ago when parents had invited me to explain the new health curriculum I was recommending for the state. As I approached the podium I noticed every person had their "Health Choices" ring binder opened to the chapter on human reproduction. One after another they told me how offensive and unacceptable this was for their children, how health was the fourth leaf of the 4-H clover, how I was ruining 4-H.

weapons of war
it would seem
are safer than books

I Can't Mend the Coral Reef

Today the water is aqua and crystal clear
fish too many to count   a school of gar gliding
like pencils of cellophane
over ripples in the sand a great barracuda
stalking a fisherman's bait   like waltzers
on a dance floor two eagle rays sway
in perfect time with the waves

I know the earth is warming
the ocean's turning acid   bleaching
the coral reef   glaciers melting costing
the polar bears their floes
red tides killing dolphins and fish
wildfires burning
turning forests into ghost towns
of cinder and smoke

But today the air is crisp in my throat
a mockingbird trills and talks in the bare
branches of the frangipani over the porch
a philodendron climbs giant leaves
around the gumbo limbo's crusty trunk
a shaving brush tree spews
the sky with little puffs of pink
a forked frigate bird soars overhead

I can get rid of plastics   eat less red meat
recycle bottles and tin   I can walk
and ride my bike   I can protest
and march in the street   I can write
to capture the jasmine's fragrance
the melody of the mockingbird   I can render
the vibrant violet of the orchids in the palms
the leathery iguana warming in the sun
the rhythm of the dancing rays   but I can't
replace the rainforest's trees or purify the sea
I can't make the glaciers refreeze
I can't mend the coral reef

The Great Blue Heron at Silver Lake

The great blue heron at Silver Lake
isn't going anywhere. Perched on the dock
with the lattice gazebo she knows she's safe.
    nine thousand border patrols
    six hundred miles of fence
The heron eyes the line of empty mansions
doors bolted shades drawn deck chairs
coiled in chains.
    airplanes
    helicopters
    a thousand military troops
She doesn't flinch
at the runner passing by or a car
rattling down the street. She creeps thin orange legs
into the reeds at the edge of the lake. She knows
she is safe.
    twelve thousand underground sensors
    Immigration and Customs Enforcement
    a concrete wall
The great blue heron pays no mind to the fluttering
cormorant wings or clamor of geese veeing for journey.
She won't fly to the border like the red knots
the sandpipers or the purple martins
who left this lake weeks ago.
    a travel ban
    tear gas and razor wire
    the National Guard
She knows she is safe
among those who know when there are enough.
Enough to wash their windows scrub their floors nanny
their children to manicure these lawns.

roofless shelters
deportations
children pulled from parent's hands
Barely rippling water the heron wades belly deep
arches her elastic neck thrusts knife beak
into prey swallows it whole. Again and again.
Sated with frogs and fishes she spans broad wings
to the sky. In rhythm with her glassy reflection
she circles the lake and returns

to claim her place atop the gazebo
with the *No Trespassing* sign.

Hay Creek Cemetery

I have been gone from here for so long
this cemetery is the only thing left.
Brown clouds swirl around the snake of cars
grinding up the gravel road. Dry grass crunches
under our shoes. Hot wind whips
hair across my face, tips
a vase of flowers, blows out
candles on the white linen cloth.

Granddaughters have planted peonies
beside my mother's plot placed
a Mayflower medallion on my father's stone.
A great grandson frolics four-year-old legs
from grave to grave among tombstones
where my brothers and I used to play.

We have come to this little country cemetery
that abuts our old farm to celebrate our parents.
To bring their ashes to where they started
their lives together on 80 acres nearly a century ago.

Like a sepia film of the Depression
our house shabby and dark, paint peeling
from my father's state-of-the-art milking parlor
the granary door swinging on a hinge. A few scrawny
chickens pecking at dandelions in the barnyard.

A field right outside my old bedroom window grows
nothing. A dingy trailer house with a clap board lean-to,
a grey metal shed, two pick up trucks parked in the dirt,
and a big yellow dog tied to a propane tank
in the field where fragrant alfalfa bloomed
in those gone summer days.

A granddaughter reads a history of our family.
The local pastor says a prayer. A grandson
places the urns. My oldest brother whispers
goodbye to our parents and to this land
I'll never walk again.

The yellow dog howls in the hot sun.

Skeletons in Old Town Key West

In January I can't tell if the bare tree
is a Royal Poinciana or a giant mango
A few doves a white capped pigeon perch
in her sprawling arms but no buds no leaves
shade the three tall houses being built beneath

Every morning through the kitchen window I search
her wide torso her pleading black branches
for signs of life   I watch an osprey soaring
overhead I listen to roosters crowing hens scratching
dry brown gravel at her roots

The carpenters start before dawn idling their
diesel trucks in front of my porch loading
trash from the teardown that left a skeleton
of the old eyebrow house once a hallmark of this town

Sawing sanding nailing balancing on the roof
in cargo shorts and steel toed boots long grey hair curling
under tee shirts tied on their heads cigarettes dangling
from their lips   progress is slow but they are building three houses
where used to be one and the humidity is heartless

By the end of March I see that this relic will not
offer up buds leaves or blossoms this spring or any other

The hurricane last September didn't kill this old queen
but four years of construction jostled her roots scraped
her bark bruised her soul   she will never unfold a flaming canopy
like the Royal Poinciana she once was

When the wood siding is nailed down the metal roof polished to a sheen the picket fence painted white and yellow hibiscus and fragrant jasmine bloom by her front door then will they chop down this tree or will they leave her skeleton to chronicle what gentrification means to a town

Osprey's Return Ghazal

Through winter's cold she will wait for you.
In March she'll mark a new date for you.

On wide wings, fly north to the tower
where windstorms lashed a new fate for you.

Rebuild with twigs from last year's frail nest,
for spring will bring your life mate to you.

Its gentle winds and briny water
make summer the perfect state for you.

Raise a new brood, fish for food, soar high.
Trust Sherri will not be late for you.

White Porcelain Vase

On my writing desk I have a white porcelain vase in the shape of a girl's head. Her eyes are closed, her lips expressionless, and her hair sculpted around her face like a Greek goddess carved in stone. This vase filled with white and yellow daisies came from friends Mike and Marybeth the day my daughter was born. My husband and I met them as graduate students working on the same research project. We cooked meals together, gardened together, drank wine together. We camped and hiked in the Adirondacks. We shared the excitement of our first child. Their baby boy born a few months later. I thought we would be friends forever. But school ended, they moved away, we moved away. We corresponded and visited a couple of times when our babies were toddlers but we divorced, they divorced. We lost touch.

This silent muse has accompanied me through many cities, many houses, into every niche I have carved out for writing. Not judging, not weighing in, just holding pencils, scissors, an antique brass letter opener, and purple and blue pens. As I look at her today I realize that, like my daughter, she is fifty years old. And despite everything she has been through—the wilted daisies, the lost friends, the divorces, the moves, she remains the same—a perfect white porcelain face.

On Moving to a Small Town

Friends thought I'd hate it, since I'd lived so long
in the city. But here, from my third floor deck,
sometimes an osprey, sometimes a bald eagle
perches high in a treetop. A red fox or a raccoon
might walk along the canal just outside
my backdoor. Not far away the ocean pulse
emits salty air, continually changes her color.
Here, just one main street, small shops,
an old-fashioned candy store. Boardwalk fragrance
of caramel corn and French Fries with vinegar.
A little theater. A shoe store owner who knows
I wear size seven and my favorite color is purple.
Here, people walk a little slower they pause
and say hello, greet my dog by his name.
I love that when I sit at my desk to write
cardinals, blue jays, little sparrows
and in summer, the hummingbirds—
come to my window.

Waiting for Sunrise

Barefoot guests tiptoed
on sand cooled by the night
murmuring *finally   finally*

orange and red flaming lanterns
lofted into the dark sky
seagulls chanted
waves whispered prayers for the sun

the minister in black robe brought
her wife and the singer
his husband

a black dog and a man watched
from a distance
the circle of friends closed in

brides linked hands
walked silently to the shore
silhouettes
against a veil of grey marble clouds

on cue at 6:04 vows spoken
rings exchanged
the sea opened her arms
lifted the veil

and the sun
sang Hallelujah
to the new day
and to the lovers

who had waited so long

They Sit Together on the Deck

holding onto the day   dinner waits

in the kitchen   they talk
about the news   how many new cases

how many died today   they admit
they are afraid they miss their children

he brings her a glass of rosè   low sun reflects gold
onto the ripples of the canal   squirrels catapult

from pine to cedar   hummingbirds sip
the red mandavilla they'd planted in the spring

cardinals *chew chew pichew*   vying for a berth
at the feeder   Linda Ronstadt's *looking forward*

to happier times drifts through warm evening air
the tabby cat curls under the table   the dog sprawls

nose under railing   they talk about
his learning to cook   her sharing

her essays and poems   how they've begun
reading the same books

they look at each other anew
seeing the one person in the world
they can talk to every single day

squirrels on branches   herons stalk the shore
fox on the bank   canal flowing to the bay

the dog and the cat who sleep in their bed
these small things

Love Poem After Thirty-Seven Years

I didn't plan to fall in love again   I was content
        with my daughter   our little green house
a short jog to city lakes   my job at the university
where you and I met

I asked you to join me on a ten-mile run
        not a date   a training for the marathon
you didn't hesitate   arrived early that Saturday morning
to run with me   and did the same the next week
and the next and then you signed up too
        every Saturday two more miles   breakfasts
at an outdoor cafe in sun baked skin and sweaty clothes

On Saturday night dinners   pasta   wine   chocolate cake
        muscles firming   endurance growing
desire escalating   we couldn't get enough
made excuses to talk at work   voltage building until
one night we both knew   you wouldn't go home

Bodies in overdrive   distance runs in the morning
house hunting in the afternoon   planning a wedding in between
For twenty-six miles   down the shore of Lake Superior
        crisp air   clear blue sky   a perfect day
to set my record time   we ran side by side
        until you got weak   and had to walk   I slowed
took your hand to cross the finish line together

We would learn to stand together at the start   kiss
good luck   and run our own pace

At thirty-seven years   our spark has gentled
         to an evenly flowing current
your lips on the back of my neck as I wash lettuce in the sink
your smile after I read you my latest poem
         a knowing look that needs no words
we go our own ways   but end always in the same place

I Write Her Name in the Sand

One week after my mother died   I run
to the boardwalk   grey ocean undistinguishable
from grey sky   colorless gulls   seashells
overturned in empty tide pools
cold wind stings my cheeks
with a stick of driftwood   I slowly etch
NORA WRIGHT 1917–2018
in giant letters in the sand

I knew she was dying when I packed
my laptop   my one good black dress   remembering
the pastor who memorialized my dad with a lofty
sermon   proving he never knew the man who
was a founder of this church   he didn't know my mother either

For three days I sat with her and watched
care attendants   nurses   social workers   hospice staff
the woman who cleaned her room   bend down
feel her forehead   touch her cheek   they told me
every day Nora would greet them with a smile and ask
how are you? where do you live? do you have children?
She'd compliment a new hairstyle a pretty shirt
thank them for coming to see her   unable to walk
stand on her own   bathe or dress herself   my mother
never complained

The director came in late at night to turn my mother
on her side   swab her dry mouth   the musician sang
In the Garden   my mother's favorite she said
The chaplain prayed
Nora told me her family loved her   keep talking
she will hear you

My mother did not open her eyes again she did not talk to me
but these caretakers   who work long hours for low wages
who watch death every day   who see all
their patients die   showed me a beautiful woman

I walk back to the boardwalk   sand fills my shoes
wind tangles my hair   regret   relief   guilt for feeling relief
and emptiness   surge like the waves to the shore
and I wonder   did I ever know who she was

I watch as her name washes out to sea

Autumnal Equinox

The sun crosses the celestial equator
both day and night are twelve hours long

Autumn colors the land gold and russet
textures the sky with cumulus clouds that wrap
sunset in crimson   push the rainstorm out to sea

Autumn infuses her crisp air with scent of jasmine
leaves crunching   the mockingbird's shrill
trill from atop a holly tree   blackbirds' loud chatter
as they swarm and gather for their journey
to warmer climes where the orioles
and osprey have already gone

I reach out to summer in her final day   I plead
for one more afternoon at the beach   one more
jacketless walk with the dog   another lazy sunset

But I know autumn must bring summer to an end
harvest her fruits   bare her deciduous trees prepare
for the shortest day of the year
the longest night   the swift glide
into the winter of my life

When You Write My Eulogy

Make it kind don't include teasing
poor Billy in the cloak room or riding
in my girlfriend's boyfriend's fast car
radio blasting tires screeching laying rubber
don't say I cried and begged to go home
and then she and I drifted apart

We'd worn matching shirtwaist dresses
and black suede shoes the first day
of eighth grade stayed up all night playing 45's
dancing to Buddy Holly and Elvis in our pajamas
and socks   I heard she married
her hot rod boyfriend senior year
but I had moved away and never saw her again

Paint me in a positive light   junior princess
in the dress review   purple ribbon at the county fair
high school honor roll   please don't mention senior
banquet when the principal announced my scholarship
after I'd skipped out to drive around in my mother's
coral Oldsmobile   smoking cigarettes   looking for boys

Gloss over getting married young   but include
a bachelor's   a master's   a daughter
who loves to read   love-ins   sit-ins
anti-war protests and bell bottom
pants   don't mention my divorce
or deferred adolescence   but apologize
for the times I was a lousy parent

For all the rest just say I loved children and dogs
and worked hard for fifty years
just say *she ran some fast races*
and wrote a few good poems

Autumnal Equinox

The sun crosses the celestial equator
both day and night are twelve hours long

Autumn colors the land gold and russet
textures the sky with cumulus clouds that wrap
sunset in crimson   push the rainstorm out to sea

Autumn infuses her crisp air with scent of jasmine
leaves crunching   the mockingbird's shrill
trill from atop a holly tree   blackbirds' loud chatter
as they swarm and gather for their journey
to warmer climes where the orioles
and osprey have already gone

I reach out to summer in her final day   I plead
for one more afternoon at the beach   one more
jacketless walk with the dog   another lazy sunset

But I know autumn must bring summer to an end
harvest her fruits   bare her deciduous trees prepare
for the shortest day of the year
the longest night   the swift glide
into the winter of my life

When You Write My Eulogy

Make it kind don't include teasing
poor Billy in the cloak room or riding
in my girlfriend's boyfriend's fast car
radio blasting tires screeching laying rubber
don't say I cried and begged to go home
and then she and I drifted apart

We'd worn matching shirtwaist dresses
and black suede shoes the first day
of eighth grade stayed up all night playing 45's
dancing to Buddy Holly and Elvis in our pajamas
and socks   I heard she married
her hot rod boyfriend senior year
but I had moved away and never saw her again

Paint me in a positive light   junior princess
in the dress review   purple ribbon at the county fair
high school honor roll   please don't mention senior
banquet when the principal announced my scholarship
after I'd skipped out to drive around in my mother's
coral Oldsmobile   smoking cigarettes   looking for boys

Gloss over getting married young   but include
a bachelor's   a master's   a daughter
who loves to read   love-ins   sit-ins
anti-war protests and bell bottom
pants   don't mention my divorce
or deferred adolescence   but apologize
for the times I was a lousy parent

For all the rest just say I loved children and dogs
and worked hard for fifty years
just say *she ran some fast races*
and wrote a few good poems

Brushing the Dog

The moment I bring out the basket with the dog brush
she thrusts her front legs up on the bed and whimpers
until I hoist her up, take off her collar, start

raking through thick black bear hair, combing
silky white belly hair
as she rolls over and lifts all four legs to the sky.

By the time I untangle her abundant tail
I have filled the trash bag with matted cottony
dog-scented hair and she

is drooling and dreaming of the greenie she knows
is reward for giving up her coat.
It is a little strange what this dog will do for me

that she won't do for you. You've always been
her alpha male. But then I won't roll over
and play dead or give up my coat for you either.

If Today

If today should be my last,
I would not regret:
giving the blue stone necklace I wanted myself
      to my daughter
writing a sentimental poem to my grandson
walking with my husband instead of running alone
stopping to watch twelve pelicans at the fishing pier
      eating their last supper.

About the Author

Sherri Wright is a member of the Rehoboth Beach Writers Guild and the Key West Poetry Guild. She lives with her husband in Rehoboth Beach, Delaware, where she walks the boardwalk, practices yoga, and volunteers for a local food rescue. Her work has appeared in *Bluebird Word, Rat's Ass Review, Delaware Beach Life, Raven's Perch,* and *Quartet*.

www.ingramcontent.com/pod-product-compliance
Lightning Source LLC
Chambersburg PA
CBHW031207160426
43193CB00008B/536